# BOOK ONE

# OPERATION TIMOTHY

CBMC
Publications
P. O. Box 3308
Chattanooga, TN 37404

The Christian Business Men's Committee is an international evangelical organization of Christian business and professional men whose primary purpose is to present Jesus Christ as Savior and Lord to other business and professional men and to train these men to carry out the Great Commission.

CBMC of USA is a nondenominational, non-profit Christian ministry supported by gifts from people committed to reaching and discipling business and professional men for Jesus Christ.

More information may be obtained by writing: Christian Business Men's Committee of USA, 1800 McCallie Avenue, Chattanooga, Tennessee 37404.

Operation Timothy was developed by CBMC for its ministry to business and professional men. It is a proven, effective strategy for building disciples.



Operation Timothy Workbook 1 - ISBN# 094-529-2015

# OPERATION TIMOTHY

## Table of Contents

*CHAPTER ONE*

# HOW TO KNOW YOU HAVE ETERNAL LIFE

You are a special person.

You are special because of God. God says you are valuable to him. He genuinely cares about you and what happens to you.

In this chapter, you will investigate four statements of God's concern for you:

- God created you.
- God knows you.
- God loves you.
- God made you part of his family.

## GOD CREATED YOU

**1.** Genesis is the book of beginnings. Chapter 1 tells us that God created the universe. Read Genesis 1:1-5. List at least three facts concerning the creation.

**2.** How did God create the world? *Read Hebrews 11:3*

**3.** Why did God create all things? *Revelation 4:11*

**4.** Why did God create you? *Isaiah 43:7*

______________________________________________

**5.** The dignity God gave man is shown by man's uniqueness, his authority, and his purpose. List some facts from Genesis 1:26-28 that indicate:

a. The uniqueness of man ______________________

______________________________________________

______________________________________________

b. The position or authority of man ______________

______________________________________________

______________________________________________

c. The purpose of man ________________________

______________________________________________

______________________________________________

## GOD KNOWS YOU

**6.** In Psalm 139:1-6 David mentions several areas of his life which God has "searched and known." List at least four of them. Then place a check mark by the areas God knows about your life.

______________________________________________

______________________________________________

______________________________________________

______________________________________________

______________________________________________

**7.** How did David respond as he realized how completely God knew him? *Psalm 139:23-24*

______________________________________________

______________________________________________

______________________________________________

**8.** What does Jesus reveal about God's detailed interest in you? *Matthew 10:29-31*

**GOD LOVES YOU**

**9.** What was God's greatest demonstration of his love? *1 John 4:9-10*

(*Manifest* means to show or make apparent; *propitiation* or *expiation* means a payment that restores favor.)

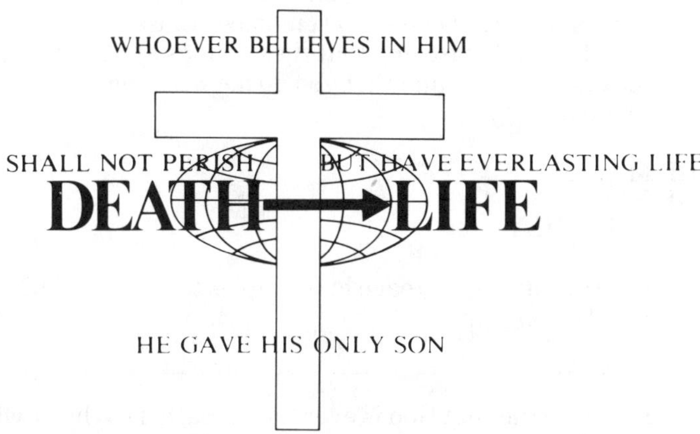


**10.** Study John 3:16 in relationship to the illustration above.

a. What did God's love cause him to do?

b. What does it mean that God "gave" his Son?

c. How can a person receive eternal life?

**11.** In John 10:9-16, Jesus compares his love and concern to the love and concern of a shepherd. According to this passage, what are some of the things he wants to give you?

**12.** Which items that you listed in question 11 are most important to you?

Take a moment to pray. Thank God for all the things you listed in question 11. Specifically remember those which mean the most to you. Praise him that these things are given to you because of Jesus, and that you do not earn them by your actions.

## GOD MADE YOU PART OF HIS FAMILY

**13.** How did Jesus teach his disciples to address God? *Matthew 6:9*

**14.** Is it true that God is everyone's Father? Why or why not? *John 8:42-44*

**15.** How is one born into God's family? *John 1:12-13*

---

> *"The importance of the assurance of faith lies in the fact that, childlike, I cannot possibly love or serve God if I do not know whether he loves and acknowledges me as his child."*
>
> —ANDREW MURRAY*

**16.** List some of the advantages of being a true child of God from Romans 8:15-17.

---

---

---

(*Abba* is a personal name for father.)

**17.** State briefly how you know God is your Father.

---

---

It is important for you as a Christian to be assured that God is your Father and that you have eternal life. Since feelings change, this assurance must ultimately depend on the word of God. "I write these things to you who believe . . . that you may know that you have eternal life" (1 John 5:13).

Below are three verses that have helped many Christians gain this assurance. You may want to memorize the verse which helps you most in this area.

> *"I tell you the truth, whoever hears my word and believes him who sent me has eternal life and will not be condemned; he has crossed over from death to life."*
>
> —JOHN 5:24

> *"And this is the testimony: God has given us eternal life, and this life is in his Son. He who has the Son has life; he who does not have the Son of God does not have life."*
>
> —1 JOHN 5:11-12

> *"Here I am! I stand at the door and knock. If anyone hears my voice and opens the door, I will go in and eat with him, and he with me."*
>
> —REVELATION 3:20

*From "The Assurance of Faith" in *The New Life* (1891).

**Remember These Points:**

- God created you for his own purpose and his glory. He gave you dignity by shaping you after his own likeness.
- God considers you to be of great value. He takes personal interest in knowing you completely.
- He loves you so intensely that he sent his Son to die for you on the cross. This demonstration of his love shows he wants to give you an eternal and abundant life.
- When God gave you this life in Jesus Christ, you were spiritually born into God's family. He is your Father. You are his child.

## NOTES

## NEXT ASSIGNMENT

Workbook Chapter:

Memory verse:

Meeting Location:

Date: Time:

Additional Notes:

*CHAPTER TWO*

# HOW TO UNDERSTAND THE WORK OF CHRIST

Many have heard about the last events of Jesus' sinless life on earth. He was condemned as a common criminal, hung from a cross until dead, and three days later he rose from the dead. But few people understand the meaning of these events.

In this chapter, you will explore Jesus' life, his death, and his resurrection.

## THE LIFE OF JESUS CHRIST

About 2,000 years ago, Jesus Christ was born in the obscure town of Bethlehem. While Jesus was an infant, Joseph and Mary took him into Egypt to escape the wrath of an irate king, Herod the Great. Then, while he was still a young child, they moved to Nazareth of Galilee.

**1.** When the angel announced his birth, what purpose did he give for Jesus coming into the world?
*Matthew 1:21; Luke 1:31-33*

______________________________

______________________________

______________________________

**2.** In what ways did Jesus develop as a youth?
*Luke 2:52*

______________________________

______________________________

**3.** What are some activities of Jesus' public ministry? *Matthew 4:23*

________________________________________________________

________________________________________________________

________________________________________________________

**4.** What was his purpose in selecting the twelve apostles? *Mark 3:14*

________________________________________________________

________________________________________________________

________________________________________________________

**5.** What characterized Jesus' leadership? *Luke 22:25-27*

________________________________________________________

How can you follow Jesus' example?_______________________

________________________________________________________

________________________________________________________

This study booklet merely touches on the events of Jesus' life. At the end of the Gospel of John we read, "Jesus did many other things as well. If every one of them were written down, I suppose that even the whole world would not have room for the books that would be written" (John 21:25). Some of the more familiar events of Jesus' life are presented in the illustration on page **11**.

## THE DEATH OF JESUS CHRIST

**6.** What did Jesus predict would happen to him? *Matthew 16:21*

________________________________________________________

________________________________________________________

**7.** What kind of death did Jesus suffer? *Matthew 27:35*

________________________________________________________

With what kind of men did he die? *Matthew 27:38*

________________________________________________________

# AN OVERVIEW OF THE LIFE OF CHRIST

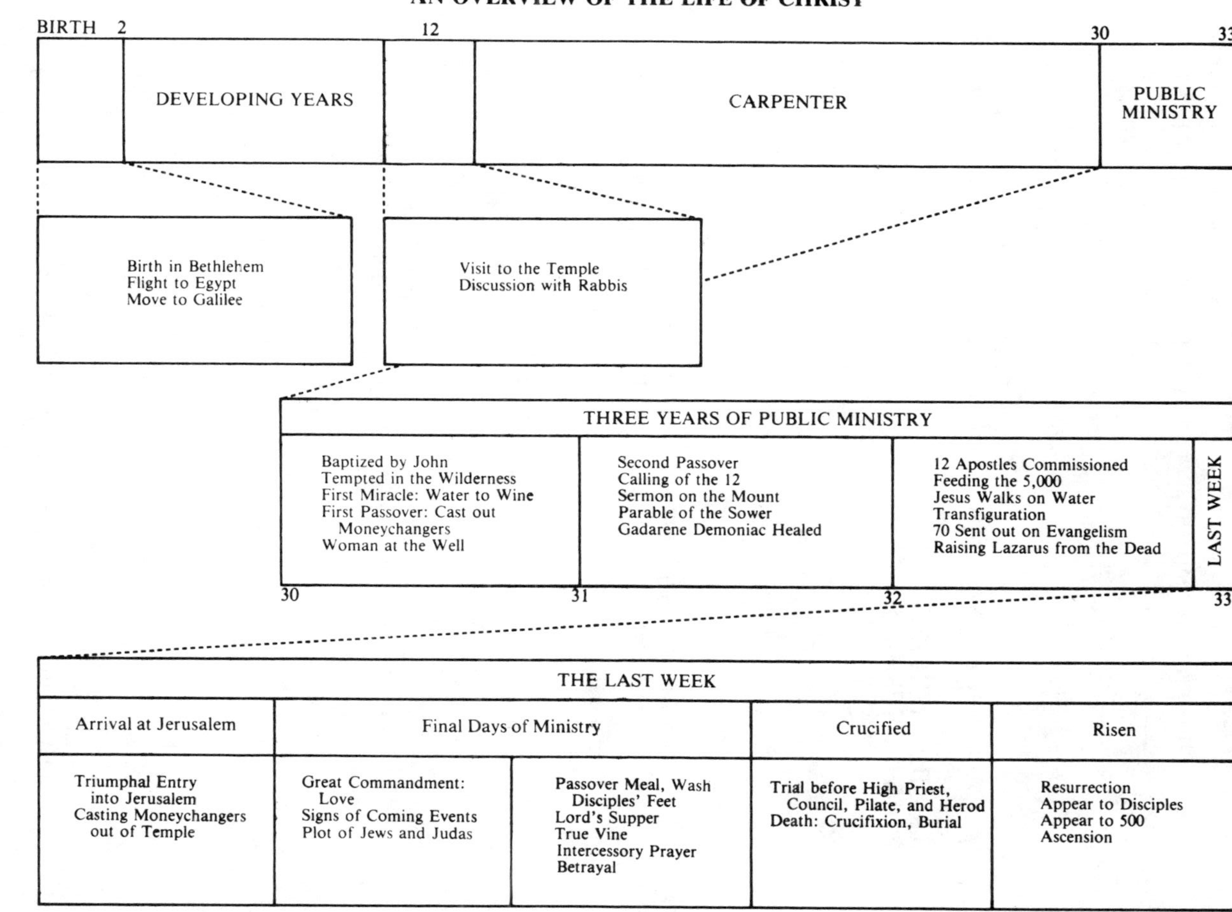

**8.** Did Jesus go to the cross voluntarily? Explain your answer. *John 10:17-18*

**9.** What is man's condition apart from Christ? *John 3:18*

**10.** Look up 1 Peter 3:18. What did Jesus do to bring condemned men to God?

**11.** Can anything be added to Christ's death to make you more acceptable to God? Why or why not? *Hebrews 10:12-14*

## THE RESURRECTION OF JESUS CHRIST

**12.** After Jesus died and was buried, what was done to secure his tomb? *Matthew 27:62-66*

**13.** Read Matthew 28:1-7. What was discovered at the tomb on the first day of the week?

What did the angel say about Jesus?

**14.** What were the soldiers bribed to say?
*Matthew 28:11-15*

> *"As a lawyer I have made a prolonged study of the evidences for the events of the first Easter Day. To me the evidence is conclusive, and over and over again in the High Court I have secured the verdict on evidence not nearly so compelling . . . . I accept [the Gospel evidence for the resurrection] unreservedly as the testimony of truthful men to facts they were able to substantiate."*
>
> —EDWARD CLARKE*

**15.** After his resurrection, Christ appeared to his disciples.

a. What was their first impression? *Luke 24:36-37*

b. What things did he do to show them he had a body?
*Luke 24:39-43*

**16.** What is the essence of the gospel message?
*1 Corinthians 15:1-5*

*As quoted by John R. W. Stott in *Basic Christianity* (London: Inter-Varsity Christian Fellowship, 1958), page 46.

**Remember These Points:**

- Jesus Christ was born in Bethlehem, raised in Galilee, and became a carpenter. He spent three years ministering to thousands and proving that he was the Christ.
- Then he was condemned to die on a cross to bear the penalty for our sin.
- After three days, Jesus rose bodily from the dead. His resurrection is a historical reality.

## NOTES

## NEXT ASSIGNMENT

Workbook Chapter:

Memory verse:

Meeting Location:

Date: Time:

Additional Notes:

*CHAPTER THREE*

# HOW TO BE SURE OF GOD'S DELIVERANCE

Man is incapable of fully understanding God. God is holy and man is sinful. To bridge the gap between God and man, God took the form of a man in Jesus Christ.

Jesus Christ is "the image of the invisible God . . . . For God was pleased to have all his fullness dwell in him" (Colossians 1:15,19).

To be the complete expression of God, Christ had to be God. To be seen and understood by man, he had to be human. Jesus Christ has a dual nature—he is the God-man.

In order to begin understanding Jesus Christ, it is necessary to explore *his deity* and *his humanity*.

## THE DEITY OF JESUS CHRIST

Some speak of Jesus Christ as a great man. To some he was the founder of a new religion. Others consider him a prophet. But Jesus himself claimed that he was God. If this claim were not true, he could not be called even a good man, but would be an imposter and a liar.

The writer of Hebrews discusses Christ's deity in chapter 1. Read this chapter before answering questions 1-4.

**1.** Jesus' superiority to the angels is shown by:

*Verses 4-5* ________________________________________

________________________________________

________________________________________

*Verse 6* ________________________________________

______________________________________________

______________________________________________

*Verses 13-14* ____________________________________

______________________________________________

______________________________________________

**2.** Look again at Hebrews 1:8-12. In the blank next to each statement below, write the number of the verse that brings out the truth stated.

Jesus is the Creator ____________________

Jesus is unchangeable ____________________

Jesus is eternal ____________________

Jesus is righteous ____________________

**3.** What is one fact about Jesus mentioned in Hebrews 1:3 that enables him to reveal God? (There is more than one fact given in this verse.)

______________________________________________

**4.** How does God address Jesus in Hebrews 1:8?

______________________________________________

In Hebrews 1:10? ____________________________________

**5.** What did Jesus claim for himself? *John 10:28-30*

______________________________________________

______________________________________________

**6.** While on earth, Jesus performed many miracles which clearly demonstrated his divine power. From the following verses in Matthew 8, list the ways Jesus showed supernatural power.

*Verse 3* ________________________________________

*Verses 6, 13* ____________________________________

*Verses 16-17* ____________________________________

*Verses 23-27* ____________________________________

**7.** What did Jesus do in John 11:39-44 that revealed his unique power?

**8.** After observing Jesus' life, power, and preaching, what did Peter conclude about him? *Matthew 16:13-16*

**9.** The chart on pages **18-19** illustrates how Jesus fulfilled prophecy. How do the verses in this chart influence your concept of who Jesus is?

**10.** Review questions 1-9. Give three reasons why you believe Jesus Christ is God.

## THE HUMANITY OF JESUS CHRIST

**11.** How is Jesus' humanity seen in the following situations?

*John 4:6* ________

*John 4:7* ________

*John 11:35* ________

# PROPHECIES ABOUT JESUS CHRIST

Fulfilled prophecy helps verify the fact that Jesus is the Christ, the Son of God. Looking at prophecies which preceded Jesus by hundreds of years and seeing how Jesus fulfilled them in every detail reveals the authenticity of his claims. The chart below is a brief list of some of the prophecies made concerning the Christ and how Jesus fulfilled them.

| TOPIC | PROPHECY | FULFILLMENT |
|---|---|---|
| Place of birth | "But you, Bethlehem Ephrathah, though you are small among the clans of Judah, out of you will come for me one who will be ruler over Israel, whose origins are from of old, from ancient times" (Micah 5:2), 700 B.C. | "Jesus was born in Bethlehem in Judea" (Matthew 2:1). |
| Born of a virgin | "The virgin will be with child and will give birth to a son, and will call him Immanuel" (Isaiah 7:14), 700 B.C. | "His mother Mary was pledged to be married to Joseph, but before they came together, she was found to be with child through the Holy Spirit" (Matthew 1:18). |
| His triumphal entry | "Rejoice greatly, O Daughter of Zion! Shout, daughter of Jerusalem! See, your King comes to you, righteous and having salvation, gentle and riding on a donkey, on a colt, the foal of a donkey" (Zechariah 9:9), 500 B.C. | "They took palm branches and went out to meet him, shouting, 'Hosanna! Blessed is he who comes in the name of the Lord! Blessed is the King of Israel!' Jesus found a young donkey and sat upon it" (John 12:13-14). |

| | | |
|---|---|---|
| Betrayed by a friend | "Even my close friend, whom I trusted, he who shared my bread, has lifted up his heel against me" (Psalm 41:9), 1000 B.C. | "Then Judas Iscariot, one of the Twelve, went to the chief priests to betray Jesus to them" (Mark 14:10). |
| His rejection | "He was despised and rejected by men . . . Like one from whom men hide their faces he was despised, and we esteemed him not" (Isaiah 53:3), 700 B.C. | "He came to that which was his own, but his own did not receive him" (John 1:11). |
| Crucified with sinners | "He . . . was numbered with the transgressors" (Isaiah 53:12), 700 B.C. | "Two robbers were crucified with him, one on his right and one on his left" (Matthew 27:38). |
| Hands and feet pierced | "They have pierced my hands and my feet" (Psalm 22:16), 1000 B.C. | "Put your finger here; see my hands. Reach out your hand and put it into my side" (John 20:27). |
| His resurrection | "You will not abandon me to the grave, nor will you let your Holy One see decay" (Psalm 16:10), 1000 B.C. | "You killed the author of life, but God raised him from the dead" (Acts 3:15). |
| His ascension | "You ascended on high" (Psalm 68:18), 1000 B.C. | "He was taken up before their very eyes, and a cloud hid him from their sight" (Acts 1:9). |

**12.** Matthew 4:1-11 is the account of a series of temptations Jesus faced.

a. In each of his three answers to Satan, Jesus used the same phrase.

What is it? ______________________________

What does it mean? ______________________________

b. Draw lines to connect the verses in Matthew 4 with the corresponding verses in Deuteronomy.

| | |
|---|---|
| Matthew 4:4 | Deuteronomy 6:13 |
| Matthew 4:7 | Deuteronomy 6:16 |
| Matthew 4:10 | Deuteronomy 8:3 |

c. What is one temptation you often face?

______________________________

______________________________

d. How can you follow Jesus' example and arm yourself against this temptation?

______________________________

______________________________

*Take time right now to pray:*

- Thank God that he understands what it is to be tempted.
- Ask him for help to overcome this temptation.
- When you fail, be sure to claim his promise: "If we confess our sins, he is faithful and just and will forgive us our sins and purify us from all unrighteousness" (1 John 1:9).
- Thank him for his mercy.

**13.** What has Jesus experienced that is common to man? *Hebrews 2:10*

______________________________

**14.** How does Jesus address believers? Why isn't he ashamed to address them this way? *Hebrews 2:11*

______________________________

______________________________

______________________________

**15.** What are some results of Jesus becoming a man? *Hebrews 2:14-15*

______

______

______

**Remember These Points:**

- Jesus Christ is the perfect image of God. As God, he has authority over the earth.
- Jesus was human, too. Many of his experiences were similar to those you have today. He suffered and was tempted. Though he never yielded, this allows him to understand when you are tempted. When you fail, he forgives as you confess your sins to him.

## NOTES

______

______

______

______

______

______

______

## NEXT ASSIGNMENT

Workbook Chapter:

Memory verse:

Meeting Location:

Date: Time:

Additional Notes:

______

*CHAPTER FOUR*

# HOW TO EXPERIENCE GOD'S FORGIVENESS

At the moment you placed your faith in Jesus Christ as your Savior, a life of obedience to God became a real possibility. The Holy Spirit set you free from the bondage of sin and death (Romans 8:2). He enables you to live a Christlike life.

> *"It is not just that we should strive to live like Jesus, but that Jesus by his Spirit should come and live in us. To have him as our example is not enough; we need him as our Savior. It is thus through his atoning death that the penalty of our sins may be forgiven; whereas it is through his indwelling Spirit that the power of our sins may be broken."*
>
> —JOHN R. W. STOTT*

As you learn more about the obedient Christian in action, remember that the Holy Spirit will help you obey.

## THE BASIS FOR OBEDIENCE

When you consider obedience to God, it is necessary to remember who he is and what he desires for you.

**1.** What do the following statements tell you about God?

a. *1 John 4:8* ____________________________________

b. *Revelation 4:11* ________________________________

---

*From *Basic Christianity* (London: Inter-Varsity Christian Fellowship, 1958), page 105.

c. How do these facts influence your obedience to God?

2. Read Deuteronomy 10:12-13

a. What did God require from Israel?

b. Why did God desire that they keep these commandments?

c. How does this apply to a Christian today?

3. What does 1 John 5:3 teach about God's commandments?

4. After reflecting on John 14:15 and 14:21, briefly state the relationship between loving God and obeying him.

## OBEDIENCE TO GOD

How do you know what God desires for your life? The Bible is God's revelation of truth, and obedience to God's word is obedience to God himself.

**5.** Psalm 119 deals with the importance of God's word. What are several ways the Bible can help you live for Christ?

*Verse 11* ______________________________

______________________________

*Verse 105* ______________________________

______________________________

*Verse 130* ______________________________

______________________________

**6.** In 2 Timothy 3:16 Paul said that the Scriptures are profitable for:

a. ______________________ (What to believe and do)

b. ______________________ (Recognizing sin)

c. ______________________ (How to change)

d. ______________________ (How to live)

This can be illustrated in the following manner:

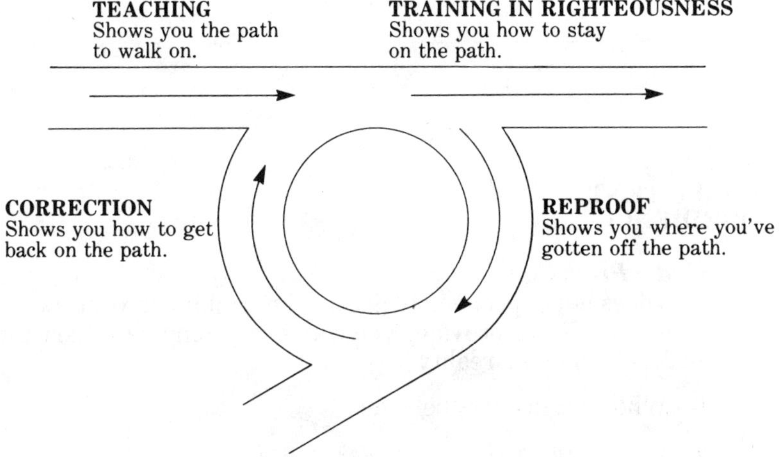

**7.** Jesus presents a vivid picture of two types of people in Matthew 7:24-27: the wise man and the foolish man. Read the passage and answer the following questions.

| | WISE MAN | FOOLISH MAN |
|---|---|---|
| On what foundation was the house built? | | |
| To what forces were both houses exposed? | | |
| What was the result? | | |
| Did this person hear God's word? | | |

How did these two men differ?

______________________________

______________________________

______________________________

______________________________

**8.** Perhaps God's word has recently made you aware of an area of your life which needs to be brought into closer obedience to God. If so, in what area?

______________________________

______________________________

## KEYS TO CONSISTENT OBEDIENCE

### *God's Provision*

God does not expect you to live an obedient life in your own strength. He has provided you with everything necessary to make obedience a reality.

**9.** Who lives in every believer?

*1 Corinthians 3:16* ______________________________

*Galatians 2:20* ______________________________

**10.** Why are Christians able to overcome their enemy in the world? *1 John 4:4*

______________________________________________

______________________________________________

______________________________________________

______________________________________________

______________________________________________

______________________________________________

**11.** In addition to his personal presence, what else has God given to help you live for him? Match the letter with the appropriate reference.

| | |
|---|---|
| ___ *2 Timothy 1:7* | a. All things that pertain to life and godliness |
| ___ *2 Peter 1:3* | b. The Scriptures |
| ___ *Romans 15:4* | c. Power, love, and self-control |

***Your Attitudes***
While God has equipped you for obedience, a key to successful use of these resources is your attitude.

**12.** What attitudes can you display in obeying God?

*Deuteronomy 26:16* ______________________________

*Psalm 40:8* ______________________________

*Luke 8:15* ______________________________

## THE PRACTICE OF OBEDIENT LIVING

The obedient Christian still faces daily struggles with temptation. How can we practice obedience and gain victory over sin? Biblical principles and examples provide the answer.

**13.** Discover the source and causes of temptation in the following verses:

a. Who is the tempter? *Matthew 4:1-3*

______________________________________________

b. Who is never the source of temptation? *James 1:13*

c. What causes you to be drawn into temptation? *James 1:14*

**14.** In Joshua 7:20-21, examine Achan's statement about his disobedience.

a. What factors contributed to his disobedience?

b. At what point could he have prevented his sin?

c. What can you learn from his error?

**15.** Using the following verses as a guide, write a brief definition of sin. *Isaiah 53:6; James 4:17; 1 John 3:4*

How does sin differ from temptation? ______________________

______________________________________________

______________________________________________

______________________________________________

______________________________________________

**16.** Consider 1 Corinthians 10:13.

a. Are the temptations you face different and perhaps more difficult than those faced by others?

______________________________________________

b. What limit does God place on temptation?

______________________________________________

______________________________________________

c. What is God sure to provide when you are tempted?

______________________________________________

______________________________________________

This verse is a promise to claim. If you memorize and review it, it will remind you to look for the way out when you are tempted.

God offers us victory and deliverance, but men sin because they often neglect the provision. Known but unconfessed sin grieves God. Although sin does not alter God's love, it does cause a break in fellowship with him.

**17.** In 1 John 1:9 we are told to. . .(Check the correct answer.)

___ feel badly about sin.

___ try to do something to make up for sin.

___ confess sin to God.

___ try to forget about sin.

Why is this important? ______________________________

______________________________________________

______________________________________________

**18.** In Psalm 32:5, David prays and confesses his sin. Write this verse in your own words.

______________________________________________

______________________________________________

______________________________________________

______________________________________________

______________________________________________

The practice of walking in victory can be pictured as follows:

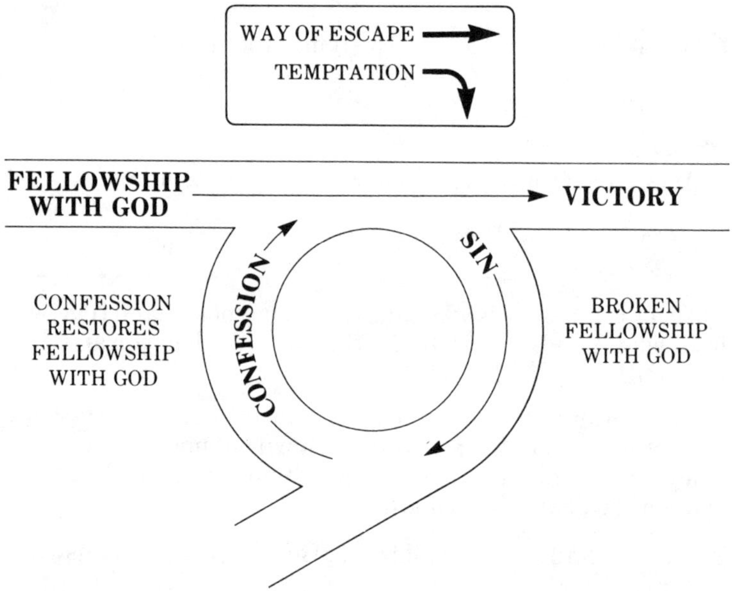

WAY OF ESCAPE →

TEMPTATION ↴

**FELLOWSHIP WITH GOD** → **VICTORY**

CONFESSION RESTORES FELLOWSHIP WITH GOD

**CONFESSION**

**SIN**

BROKEN FELLOWSHIP WITH GOD

**19.** In what practical ways can you avoid falling into temptation? *Proverbs 4:13-15*

______________________________________________

______________________________________________

______________________________________________

______________________________________________

**20.** What two steps indicated in James 4:7 will help you walk in victory?

TO SUBMIT TO GOD you must yield your will to God's will. TO RESIST THE DEVIL you must use God's provision for victory.

**21.** These questions about sin and temptation probably remind you of the daily conflict you experience.

a. Review question 8. What is the root problem in the area you recorded?

b. How does the temptation to disobey God in this area begin to show itself?

c. What steps can you take to avoid these beginnings?

> *"Live by the Spirit, and you will not gratify the desires of your sinful nature."*
>
> —GALATIANS 5:16

**Remember These Points:**

- Your obedience to God is based on the fact that he is your Creator. You obey him because of who he is.
- God reveals his standards through the Scriptures.
- To the extent that you appropriate God's provision for victory, you can experience a life of obedience.
- You are not immune, however, from temptation and sin. Sin does not negate God's love for you, but it does break your fellowship with him. Confession restores that fellowship.

## NOTES

## NEXT ASSIGNMENT

Workbook Chapter:

Memory verse:

Meeting Location:

Date: Time:

Additional Notes:

*CHAPTER FIVE*

# HOW TO LIVE BY THE POWER OF THE HOLY SPIRIT

The Bible explains what kind of relationship Christians can have with the Holy Spirit.

## WHO IS THE HOLY SPIRIT?

**1.** What activities or characteristics of the Holy Spirit are mentioned in the following verses?

*Acts 13:2* ____________________

*1 Corinthians 2:10* ____________________

*1 Corinthians 2:12-13* ____________________

*1 Corinthians 12:11* ____________________

*Ephesians 4:30* ____________________

Do these verses indicate that the Holy Spirit is a real person (though not physical)? Explain.

____________________

____________________

____________________

In the Bible, the Holy Spirit has several names, including Comforter, Spirit of Truth, Spirit of Christ, Spirit of Jesus, and Spirit of God.

**2.** What indications are there in the following verses that the Holy Spirit is God?

*Genesis 1:2* ____________________

*Hebrews 9:14* ____________________

*Psalm 139:7-8* ____________________

**3.** When Ananias and Sapphira forfeited their lives (Acts 5:1-10), to whom had they lied?

*Verse 3* ____________________

*Verse 4* ____________________

> THE TRINITY
>
> God exists as three persons (referred to as the Trinity)—yet he is one. The three persons of the Trinity are God the Father, God the Son, and God the Holy Spirit. These three are one in substance, and function in perfect harmony.
>
> The human mind cannot fully comprehend God, especially his revelation of himself as the Trinity. Yet we see unity with diversity in all parts of God's creation, all of which to a limited degree illustrate God's marvelous nature: one God in three persons.
>
> - The Father is God invisible—John 1:18.
> - The Son is God revealed—John 1:14-18, Hebrews 1:1-4.
> - The Holy Spirit is God working in men—John 16:8; 1 Corinthians 2:10-11 and 6:19-20.
>
> (Other passages that teach about the Trinity are: Matthew 3:16-17 and 28:19; John 14:16; 2 Corinthians 13:14; and 1 Peter 1:2.)

## WHO HAS THE HOLY SPIRIT?

**4.** How is the Holy Spirit involved in every conversion?

*John 3:5-6* ____________________

____________________

*Ephesians 1:13-14* ____________________

*Titus 3:5* ____________________

**5.** What has happened to every member of the body of Christ? *1 Corinthians 12:13*

**6.** Read Romans 8:9-14. What statements indicate that every believer has received the Holy Spirit?

**7. In spite of their imperfect lives, of what are believers in Corinth reminded?** ***1 Corinthians 3:16***

## THE WORK OF THE HOLY SPIRIT

**8.** Read John 16:7-15.

a. What is the Spirit of God doing today? *Verses 8-11*

b. What is he doing for believers? *Verse 13*

c. Who or what does he emphasize? *Verses 14-15*

**9.** Read Galatians 5:19-25. Notice the works (plural) of the flesh as contrasted with the fruit (singular) of the Spirit. Why do you think the word *fruit* is singular although several items are mentioned? (Compare with John 15:5.)

Just as light diffuses into a rainbow of colors when it shines through a prism, so the pure life of Christ can be displayed in your life by an array of Christian virtues.

**10.** The victorious Christian life is the subject of Romans 8. How does the Holy Spirit help you live in victory?

*Verse 2*

*Verse 14*

*Verse 16*

*Verse 26*

**11.** What role did the Holy Spirit play in Paul's missionary work?

*Acts 13:2-4*

*Acts 16:6-7*

*1 Corinthians 2:4*

**12.** What are two conflicting natures in your life? *Galatians 5:16-17*

Who should control your life?

Here is one illustration of the power which results from the union of the Holy Spirit with the believer:

> *"I have in my hand a piece of lead. I hold it over a pool of water, and relax my grip. The lead is drawn irresistibly earthwards and sinks to the bottom of the pool. It has been mastered by the law of gravitation. I take the same piece of lead, attach it to a piece of wood and drop it into the pool. Now it floats. No change has taken place in the nature or tendency of the lead, nor has the law of gravitation ceased to function, but through its union with the wood, it has been mastered by a stronger law, the law governing floating bodies, and has been emancipated from the downward pull of gravitation."*
>
> —J. OSWALD SANDERS*

**13.** Whom does the Holy Spirit glorify? *John 16:13-14*

**14.** What is the "sword" of the Spirit? *Ephesians 6:17*

**15.** What effect does the word of God have in the believer? *Hebrews 4:12*

**16.** What is one activity in which the Holy Spirit helps you? How? *Romans 8:26*

*From *The Holy Spirit and His Gifts* (Grand Rapids, Michigan: Zondervan Publishing House, 1940), page 57.

**17.** What were some of the disciples' activities after being filled with the Holy Spirit? *Acts 2:42*

______________________________________________

______________________________________________

______________________________________________

**18.** In Acts 1:8, Jesus used the expression "you will" twice. He made both of these statements in conjunction with the Holy Spirit coming on the disciples. What two statements did he make?

______________________________________________

______________________________________________

How does the Holy Spirit help you in witnessing?

______________________________________________

______________________________________________

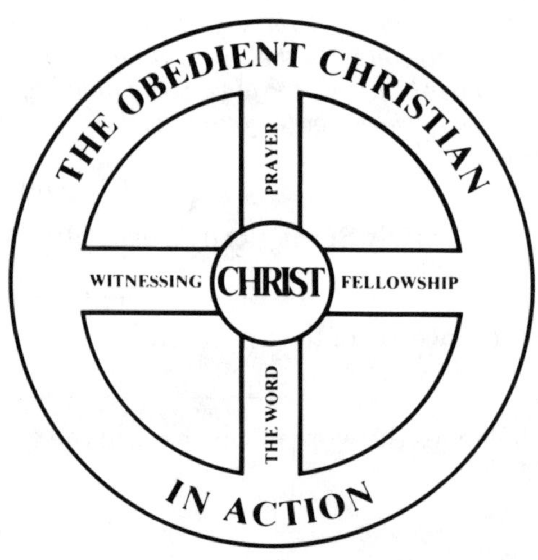


The Wheel Illustration is a helpful way to remember these basic truths about the Spirit-filled life. It is a Christ-centered life. The Holy Spirit focuses your attention on *Christ* and empowers you to live a life of *obedience* to him. *God's word* and *prayer* build you up in a relationship with Christ so he can live through you and reach others through *fellowship* and *witnessing.* Without drawing attention to himself, the Holy Spirit shapes each activity into an avenue of spiritual blessing.

**19.** Read Acts 4:31-33. List examples of the principles from the Wheel which are demonstrated by the disciples in this passage.

### YOUR RESPONSIBILITY

**20.** Read Ephesians 5:18-21.

a. What is God's commandment concerning the Holy Spirit? *Verse 18*

b. List several results of being filled with the Spirit. *Verses 19-21*

**21. What is being filled with the Holy Spirit compared to in Ephesians 5:18?**

**Why is this comparison used?**

**22.** What are you warned against in your relationship to the Holy Spirit?

*1 Thessalonians 5:19* ________________________________

*Ephesians 4:30* ________________________________

**23.** Look at the verses surrounding Ephesians 4:30.

a. What are some of the things that grieve the Holy Spirit?

________________________________

________________________________

________________________________

b. Is there anything in your life that grieves the Holy Spirit?

________________________________

________________________________

________________________________

c. What steps do you need to take?

________________________________

________________________________

________________________________

________________________________

**Remember These Points:**

Review the chapter subtopics and use them as an outline to write your own summary of the chapter here and on the next page.

________________________________

________________________________

________________________________

________________________________

________________________________

________________________________

________________________________

________________________________

## NOTES

## NEXT ASSIGNMENT

Workbook Chapter:

Memory verse:

Meeting Location:

Date: Time:

Additional Notes:

*CHAPTER SIX*

# HOW TO COMMUNICATE WITH GOD

Communication is essential for any growing relationship, including our relationship with God. Prayer is our means of communicating with him.

When you pray, the Holy Spirit helps you know what to say and how to say it (Romans 8:26-27).

> *"The Spirit links himself with us in our praying and pours his supplications into our own. We may master the technique of prayer and understand its philosophy; we may have unlimited confidence in the veracity and validity of the promises concerning prayer. We may plead them earnestly. But if we ignore the part played by the Holy Spirit, we have failed to use the master key."*
>
> J. OSWALD SANDERS*

## PRAYER— YOUR COMMUNICATION WITH GOD

**1.** As a believer in Christ you have been given a special opportunity, according to Hebrews 4:16. What is it and why was it given to you?

____________________________________________

____________________________________________

*From *Spiritual Leadership* (Chicago: Moody Press, 1967), page 79.

**2.** Because God is the believer's refuge, what are you told to do? *Psalm 62:8*

_______________________________________________

_______________________________________________

_______________________________________________

How does 1 Thessalonians 5:17 relate to this verse?

_______________________________________________

_______________________________________________

_______________________________________________

**3.** Different types of prayer are necessary to communicate the variety of thoughts you want to express. Match each reference with the corresponding type of prayer.

*Psalm 38:18* *Hebrews 13:15* *James 1:5* *Ephesians 5:20* *1 Samuel 12:23*

Praise (for who God is) ______________

Thanksgiving (for what he has done) ______________

Confession ______________

Prayer for others ______________

Prayer for personal needs ______________

## THE BENEFITS OF PRAYER

Not only do Christians have the privilege of talking with God about everything, they also experience great benefits from their communion with God.

**4.** What truth do you find both in Jeremiah 33:3 and Ephesians 3:20?

_______________________________________________

_______________________________________________

**5.** What result did the psalmist experience when he prayed? *Psalm 34:4*

_______________________________________________

What are some fears you can discuss with God?

______________________________

______________________________

______________________________

**6.** Paul wrote in Philippians 4:6-7 about a powerful key to freedom from anxiety.

a. What are you to do? ______________________________

______________________________

b. Why do you feel God is interested in every area of your life?

______________________________

______________________________

______________________________

c. What is God's promise? ______________________________

d. In what area can you immediately begin to apply this truth?

______________________________

______________________________

______________________________

## CONDITIONS OF PRAYER

**7.** What conditions of prayer do you find in the following verses?

*Psalm 66:18* ______________________________

*Matthew 21:22* ______________________________

*John 15:7* ______________________________

*John 16:24* ______________________________

*I John 5:14-15* ______________________________

Even when conditions are met, it sometimes appears as if God is not answering prayer. But remember that "No" and "Wait" are as much of an answer as "Yes."

**8.** Consider Jesus' pattern for prayer in Matthew 6:9-13.

a. How does the prayer begin? Why is this important?

b. Which requests are God-centered?

c. Which requests are man-centered?

d. In what specific ways can this pattern for praying help you pray?

## FOR WHOM DO YOU PRAY?

**9.** What did Paul desire for those who didn't know Christ? *Romans 10:1*

What did he do about it?

**10.** Read 1 Timothy 2:1-4. What groups of people should you pray for? Why?

**11.** What does the Lord desire you to pray for?
*Matthew 9:37-38*

______________________________________________

______________________________________________

Why do you feel this is important?

______________________________________________

______________________________________________

______________________________________________

______________________________________________

**12.** How do you usually react when you have been intentionally mistreated by someone? Place an "X" by your first response.

___ To become angry with him

___ To think of a way to get even

___ To make an excuse for him and try to forget it

___ To pray for him

___ To forgive but not forget

Other: ______________________________________

Examine Luke 6:28, then circle the correct response.

**13.** Using Paul's prayer in Ephesians 3:14-21 as a guideline, list some requests you could pray for others and for yourself.

______________________________________________

______________________________________________

______________________________________________

______________________________________________

______________________________________________

______________________________________________

______________________________________________

______________________________________________

______________________________________________

Have you been using a prayer list? A list can help you remember things you might otherwise forget to pray about. It can include:

- Your family
- Your non-Christian friends and acquaintances
- Your pastor and church
- Missionaries and Christian workers you know
- Those who oppose you
- Governmental authorities
- Your personal needs
- Ten most wanted card

**DAILY CONVERSATION WITH GOD**

**14.** What attitudes can you have in coming to God?

*Psalm 27:8* ______________________________

*Psalm 46:10* ______________________________

*Psalm 63:1* ______________________________

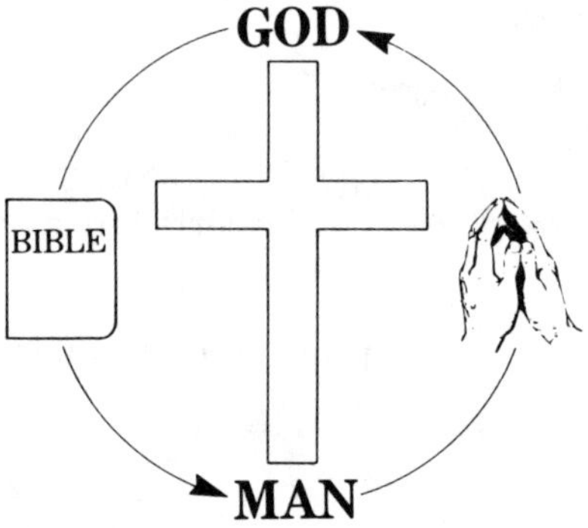

GOD

BIBLE

MAN

What truths are illustrated by this diagram?

______________________________

______________________________

______________________________

______________________________

______________________________

______________________________

**15.** Examine Luke 10:38-42. You can make several observations from this passage which relate to spending time with Jesus Christ.

a. Contrast the activities of Mary and Martha.

| MARY | MARTHA |
|---|---|
| | |

b. Which one did Jesus commend and why?

c. Like Martha, you may be easily distracted by many things. What activities might distract you from meeting with God?

d. What can you do to overcome these distractions?

**16. From what you have already learned in *Operation Timothy,* record several reasons why you need to spend daily time with God—meditating on his word and conversing with him in prayer.**

**Remember These Points:**

- God has provided prayer as the means of communicating directly with him, through Jesus Christ.
- Prayer releases us from fear and worry.
- The Scriptures provide numerous patterns and examples for our prayer.
- God *desires* your fellowship, and you *need* to grow in your relationship with him. So regular times alone with God for the purpose of fellowship are vitally necessary.

---

# Seven Minutes with God*

by Robert D. Foster

It was in 1882 on the campus of Cambridge University that the world was first given the slogan:

"Remember the morning watch."

Students like Hooper and Thornton found their days "loaded" with studies, lectures, games and bull sessions. Enthusiasm and activity were the order of the day. These dedicated men soon discovered a flaw in their spiritual armor—a small crack which if not soon closed, would bring disaster.

They sought an answer and came up with a scheme they called the morning watch—a plan to spend the first minutes of a new day alone with God, praying and reading the Bible.

The morning watch sealed the crack. It enshrined a truth so often obscured by the pressure of ceaseless activity that it needs daily rediscovery: To know God, it is necessary to spend consistent time with Him.

The idea caught fire. "A remarkable period of religious blessing" followed, and culminated in the departure of the Cambridge Seven, a band of prominent athletes and men of wealth and education, for missionary service. They gave up everything to go out to China for Christ.

But these men found that getting out of bed in time for the morning watch was as difficult as it was vital. Thornton was determined to turn indolence into discipline. He invented an automatic, foolproof cure for laziness. It was a contraption set up by his bed: "The vibration of an alarm clock set fishing tackle in motion, and the sheets, clipped to the line, moved swiftly into the air off the sleeper's body."

Thornton wanted to get up to meet his God!

The intimacy of communion with Christ must be recaptured in the morning quiet time. Call it what you want—the quiet time, personal devotions, the morning watch, or individual worship—these holy minutes at the start of each day explain the inner secret of Christianity. It's the golden thread that ties every great man of God together—from Moses to David Livingstone, the prophet Amos to Billy Graham—rich and poor, businessmen and

*Used by permission of The Navigators

military personnel. Every man who ever became somebody for God has this at the core of his priorities: time alone with God!

David says in Psalm 57:7, "My heart is fixed, O God, my heart is fixed." A fixed and established heart produces stability in life. Few men in the Christian community have this heart and life. One of the missing links has been a workable plan on how to begin and maintain a morning watch.

I want to suggest that in order to get under way, you start with seven minutes. Perhaps you could call it a daily "Seven-Up." Five minutes may be too short, and ten minutes for some is a little too long at first.

Are you willing to take seven minutes every morning? Not five mornings out of seven, not six days out of seven—but seven days out of seven! Ask God to help you: "Lord, I want to meet You the first thing in the morning for at least seven minutes. Tomorrow when the alarm clock goes off at 6:15 a.m., I have an appointment with You."

Your prayer might be, "Morning by morning, O Lord, You hear my voice; morning by morning I lay my requests before You and wait in expectation" (Psalm 5:3).

How do you spend these seven minutes? After getting out of bed and taking care of your personal needs, you will want to find a quiet place and there with your Bible enjoy the solitude of seven minutes with God.

Invest the first 30 seconds preparing your heart. Thank Him for the good night of sleep and the opportunities of this new day. "Lord, cleanse my heart so You can speak to me through the Scriptures. Open my heart. Fill my heart. Make my mind alert, my soul active, and my heart responsive. Lord, surround me with Your presence during this time. Amen."

Now take four minutes to read the Bible. Your greatest need is to hear some word from God. Allow the Word to strike fire in your heart. Meet the Author!

One of the Gospels is a good place to begin reading. Start with the Book of Mark. Read consecutively—verse after verse, chapter after chapter. Don't race, but avoid stopping to do a Bible study on some word, thought, or theological problem which presents itself. Read for the pure joy of reading and allowing God to speak—perhaps just 20 verses, or maybe a complete chapter. When you have finished

Mark, start the Gospel of John. Soon you'll want to go ahead and read the entire New Testament.

After God has spoken through His Book, then speak to Him—in prayer. You now have two and a half minutes left for fellowship with Him in four areas of prayer that you can remember by the word ACTS.

A—*Adoration.* This is the purest kind of prayer because it's all for God—there's nothing in it for you. You don't barge into the presence of royalty. You begin with the proper salutation. So worship Him. Tell the Lord that you love Him. Reflect on His greatness, His power, His majesty, and sovereignty!

C—*Confession* follows. Having seen Him you now want to be sure every sin is cleansed and forsaken. Confession comes from a root word meaning "to agree together with." Apply this to prayer. It means to agree with God. Something happened yesterday you called a slight exaggeration—God calls it a lie! You call it strong language—God calls it swearing. You call it telling the truth about somebody in the church—God calls it gossip. "If I regard iniquity in my heart, the Lord will not hear me" (Psalm 66:18).

T—*Thanksgiving.* Express your gratitude to God. Think of several specific things to thank Him for: your family, your business, your church and ministry responsibilities—even thank Him for hardships. "In everything give thanks: for this is the will of God in Christ Jesus concerning you" (1 Thessalonians 5:18).

S—*Supplication.* This means to "ask for, earnestly and humbly." This is the part of your prayer life where you make your petitions known to Him. Ask for others, then for yourself. Why not include other people around the world, such as missionaries, students studying abroad, friends in distant places, and above all the people of many lands who have yet to hear about Jesus Christ.

Let's put these seven minutes together:

| | |
|---|---|
| ½ | Prayer for guidance (Psalm 143:8) |
| 4 | Reading the Bible (Psalm 119:18) |
| 2½ | Prayer |
| | Adoration (1 Chronicles 29:11) |
| | Confession (1 John 1:9) |
| | Thanksgiving (Ephesians 5:20) |
| | Supplication (Matthew 7:7) |

---

7 minutes

This is simply a guide. Very soon you will discover that it is impossible to spend only seven minutes with the Lord. An amazing thing happens—seven minutes become 20, and it's not long before you're spending 30 precious minutes with Him. Do not become devoted to the habit, but to the Savior.

Do it not because other men are doing it—not as a spiritless duty every morning, nor merely as an end in itself, but because God has granted the priceless privilege of fellowship with Himself. Covenant with Him now to guard, nourish, and maintain your morning watch of seven minutes.

## NOTES

## NEXT ASSIGNMENT

Workbook Chapter:

Memory verse:

Meeting Location:

Date: Time:

Additional Notes:

# PRAYER REQUESTS

| Date | Request | Update/Answer Date |
| --- | --- | --- |

## Assurance of Forgiveness NIV

I John 1:9

If we confess our sins, he is faithful and just and will forgive us our sins and purify us from all unrighteousness.

*4* I John 1:9

## Fruit of the Holy Spirit NIV

Galatians 5:22-23

But the fruit of the Spirit is love, joy, peace, patience, kindness, goodness, faithfulness, gentleness and self-control. Against such things there is no law.

*5* Galatians 5:22-23

## Assurance of Answered Prayer NIV

Philippians 4:6-7

Do not be anxious about anything, but in everything, by prayer and petition, with thanksgiving, present your requests to God. And the peace of God, which transcends all understanding, will guard your hearts and your minds in Christ Jesus.

*6* Philippians 4:6-7

## Assurance of Salvation NIV

I John 5:11-13

And this is the testimony: God has given us eternal life, and this life is in his Son. He who has the Son has life; he who does not have the Son of God does not have life. I write these things to you who believe in the name of the Son of God so that you may know that you have eternal life.

*1* I John 5:11-13

## The Work of Christ NIV

Romans 5:8

But God demonstrates his own love for us in this: While we were still sinners, Christ died for us.

*2* Romans 5:8

## Assurance of Deliverance NIV

I Corinthians 10:13

No temptation has seized you except what is common to man. And God is faithful; he will not let you be tempted beyond what you can bear. But when you are tempted, he will also provide a way out so that you can stand up under it.

*3* I Corinthians 10:13

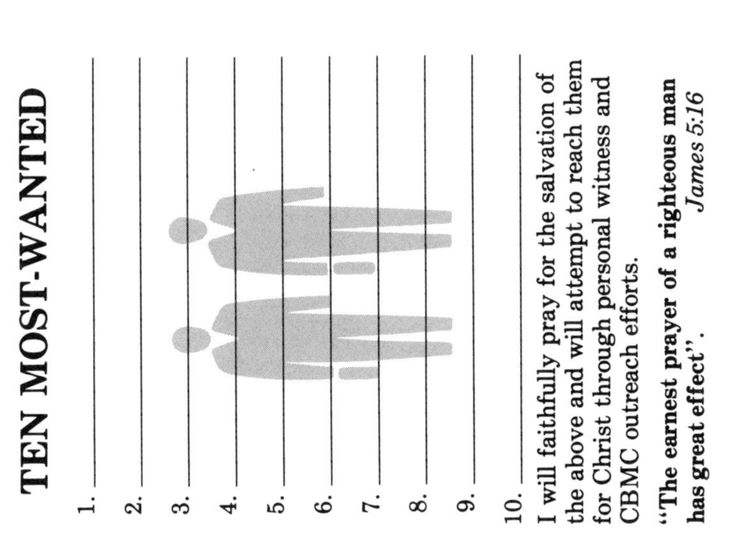

## Assurance of Salvation

KJV

I John 5:11-13

And this is the record, that God hath given to us eternal life, and this life is in his Son. He that hath the Son hath life; and he that hath not the Son of God hath not life. These things have I written unto you that believe on the name of the Son of God: that ye may know that ye have eternal life, and that ye may believe on the name of the Son of God.

*1* I John 5:11-13

## Assurance of Forgiveness

KJV

I John 1:9

If we confess our sins, he is faithful and just to forgive us our sins, and to cleanse us from all unrighteousness.

*4* I John 1:9

## The Work of Christ

KJV

Romans 5:8

But God commendeth his love toward us, in that, while we were yet sinners, Christ died for us.

*2* Romans 5:8

## Fruit of The Holy Spirit

KJV

Galatians 5:22-23

But the fruit of the Spirit is love, joy, peace, longsuffering, gentleness, goodness, faith, meekness, temperance: against such there is not law.

*5* Galatians 5:22-23

## Assurance of Deliverance

KJV

I Corinthians 10:13

There hath no temptation taken you but such as is common to man: but God is faithful, who will not suffer you to be tempted above that ye are able; but will with the temptation also make a way to escape, that ye may be able to bear it.

*3* I Corinthians 10:13

## Assurance of Answered Prayer

KJV

Philippians 4:6-7

Be careful for nothing; but in every thing by prayer and supplication with thanksgiving let your requests be made known unto God. And the peace of God, which passeth all understanding, shall keep your hearts and minds through Christ Jesus.

*6* Philippians 4:6-7